I0815085

DISCOVERING THE UNITED STATES

Nebraska

BY JOANNE MATTERN

Kids Core

An Imprint of Abdo Publishing

abdobooks.com

abdobooks.com

Published by Abdo Publishing, a division of ABDO, PO Box 398166, Minneapolis, Minnesota 55439.

Printed in China.
052024
092024

Cover Photo: Zack Frank/Shutterstock Images
Interior Photos: Quang Trung Art/Shutterstock Images, 4–5; Brian Lasenby/Shutterstock Images, 6 (top left); Ann Cantelow/Shutterstock Images, 6 (top right); Alexei Korshunov/Shutterstock Images, 6 (bottom left); Daniel Prudek/Shutterstock Images, 6 (bottom right); Shutterstock Images, 9; Ryan McGinnis/Moment/Getty Images, 10; Jerry Mennenga/ZUMA Press, Inc./Alamy Live News/Alamy, 12–13; Bettmann/Getty Images, 14, 17; Weldon Schloneger/Shutterstock Images, 18; iStockphoto, 20–21, 26, 28 (top left); Zack Frank/Shutterstock Images, 23, 29 (bottom); Mihai Andritoiu/Shutterstock Images, 24; Red Line Editorial, 28 (top right), 29 (top); Daniel Stephen Hakes/Shutterstock Images, 28 (bottom)

Editor: Laura Stickney
Series Designer: Katharine Hale

Library of Congress Control Number: 2023949357

Publisher's Cataloging-in-Publication Data

Names: Mattern, Joanne, author.
Title: Nebraska / by Joanne Mattern
Description: Minneapolis, Minnesota: Abdo Publishing, 2025 | Series: Discovering the United States | Includes online resources and index.
Identifiers: ISBN 9781098293970 (lib. bdg.) | ISBN 9798384913245 (ebook)
Subjects: LCSH: U.S. states--Juvenile literature. | Nebraska--History--Juvenile literature. | Midwest States--Juvenile literature. | Physical geography--United States--Juvenile literature.
Classification: DDC 973--dc23

All population data taken from:
"Estimates of Population by Sex, Race, and Hispanic Origin: April 1, 2020 to July 1, 2022." *US Census Bureau, Population Division*, June 2023, census.gov.

CONTENTS

The bones of ancient mammoths have been discovered throughout Nebraska.

CHAPTER 1

Archie the Mammoth

In 1921, Henry Kariger was on his ranch in Nebraska. He noticed his chickens scratching at something white in the dirt. He took a closer look. It turned out to be a bunch of bones. Kariger dug up the bones. He displayed them at the 1922 Nebraska State Fair.

Nebraska Facts

DATE OF STATEHOOD
March 1, 1867

CAPITAL
Lincoln

POPULATION
1,967,923

AREA
77,348 square miles
(200,330 sq km)

STATE BIRD

Western meadowlark

STATE TREE

Cottonwood

STATE FLOWER

Goldenrod

STATE INSECT

Honeybee

Each US state has a different population, size, and capital city. States also have state symbols.

Dr. Erwin Barbour worked for the University of Nebraska State Museum. He realized the bones were the **fossil** of a mammoth. This is a type of ancient elephant. The skeleton was nearly complete. It was 14 feet (4 m) tall and more than 25 feet (8 m) long. Barbour bought the bones. He displayed them at the museum. Later, people named the skeleton Archie.

Scientists believe Archie and other mammoths roamed Nebraska around 30,000 years ago. Archie is just one of many ancient animal fossils found in Nebraska. Today, visitors can see Archie at the University of Nebraska State Museum. He is in the Hall of Elephants.

Nebraska's Land

Nebraska is in the US region known as the Midwest. South Dakota borders the state to the north. Missouri and Iowa lie to the east.

Kansas borders Nebraska to the south, and Colorado borders it to the southwest. Wyoming lies to the west. The top western part of Nebraska stretches into a long, thin area. It is called the panhandle.

Nebraska has a very flat landscape. It is part of the Great Plains. This is an area of flat, dry land in the Midwest. Much of Nebraska's

Great American Desert

In the 1820s, some people believed the Great Plains were unfit for human life. The flat, treeless area was different from land in the eastern United States. Many Americans believed the plains were bad for farming. They called the area the Great American Desert. Most people didn't settle there until the late 1800s.

The Nebraska Sand Hills region features grassy hills. Many types of animals and plants live there.

land includes grasslands and prairies. Northern Nebraska is home to the Sand Hills. This area features low hills and valleys.

Several major rivers run through Nebraska. They include the Platte River, Missouri River, and Niobrara River. The state's largest body of water is Lake McConaughy.

Nebraska is part of a region known as Tornado Alley. States in this area are more likely to experience tornadoes than other states.

Nebraska's Climate

Nebraska has four seasons. In the western part of the state, the climate is dry. Eastern Nebraska is much wetter. This region gets more than twice the amount of rain and snow as the panhandle.

The panhandle receives around 15 inches (38 cm) of rain and snow each year. Summers in the region are hot and **humid**.

Nebraska is known for its extreme weather. The state often has severe storms in spring and summer. These include thunderstorms and tornadoes. In winter, blizzards sweep across the state. **Droughts** are also common in some areas.

Further Evidence

Visit the website below. Does it give any new information about Nebraska that wasn't mentioned in Chapter One?

Nebraska

abdocorelibrary.com/discovering-nebraska

Members of the Winnebago Tribe host an annual powwow in Winnebago, Nebraska. The event features traditional American Indian music and dancing.

CHAPTER 2

The People of Nebraska

People have been living in Nebraska for more than 10,000 years. Several American Indian nations have lived in the state. They include the Omaha, Ioway, Sioux, and Arapaho nations.

Settlers often passed through Nebraska while traveling across the Great Plains. Many rode in covered wagons pulled by horses or oxen.

Immigration

In the late 1600s and early 1700s, European settlers arrived in Nebraska. Some were French and Spanish **fur trappers**. By 1800, French settlers gained control of the area. The US government purchased a large amount of land from France in 1803. This included Nebraska.

Soon, more settlers began moving to Nebraska. To make room for the settlers, the US government forced many American Indians to leave their land. It made many nations, including the Omaha and Fox, move to **reservations**. In the 1800s and 1900s, new immigrants from eastern and central Europe came to the state.

Today, Nebraska's population is about 77 percent white. It is 12 percent Hispanic or Latino and 5 percent Black. About 3 percent of Nebraskans are Asian. Two percent are American Indian.

Culture

Nebraska is known for its history of American settlement. Famous writer Willa Cather lived in the state. She wrote about life on the Great Plains in the 1800s. Several of her books take place in Nebraska, including *My Ántonia*.

Sports are another part of Nebraska's culture. College football is a very popular sport.

Authors

Many authors have lived in Nebraska. Willa Cather and Mari Sandoz wrote about the hardships that settlers faced. Writer Susette La Flesche, also called Inshata Theumba, belonged to the Omaha Tribe of Nebraska. She wrote books and articles about American Indians and their rights.

Willa Cather lived in Red Cloud, Nebraska. She graduated from the University of Nebraska in 1895.

The University of Nebraska Cornhuskers is a well-known football team in the state.

Nebraska's culture can also be experienced through its food. Nebraska is known for foods produced in the state, such as corn and steak. Runzas are another popular food. They are bread pockets filled with ground beef, cabbage, and cheese. They were likely introduced by immigrants from central and eastern Europe.

Nebraska is one of the country's top corn producers. The state is even called the Cornhusker State.

Industry

Farming is a big industry in Nebraska. Farmers raise cattle and hogs. They grow corn, soybeans, and wheat. Other important industries include health care and oil drilling. Many Nebraskans work in **manufacturing** too.

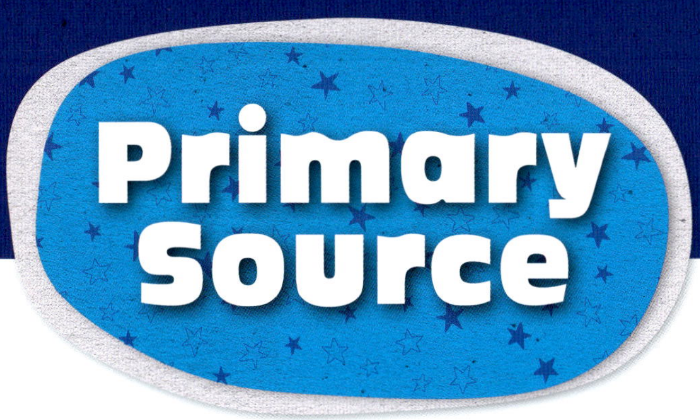

In 2023, a statue of Willa Cather was placed in the US Capitol building in Washington, DC. Ashley Olson works for the National Willa Cather Center in Red Cloud. She said:

> Many of [Cather's] most well-known stories are about Nebraska and its people. I hope her representation in our US Capitol will encourage even more readers to discover the beauty and complexity of her writing.

Source: "Cather Featured in Statuary Hall." *University of Nebraska–Lincoln*, 5 June 2023, news.unl.edu. Accessed 19 Dec. 2023.

What's the Big Idea?

What is this quote's main idea? Explain how the main idea is supported by details.

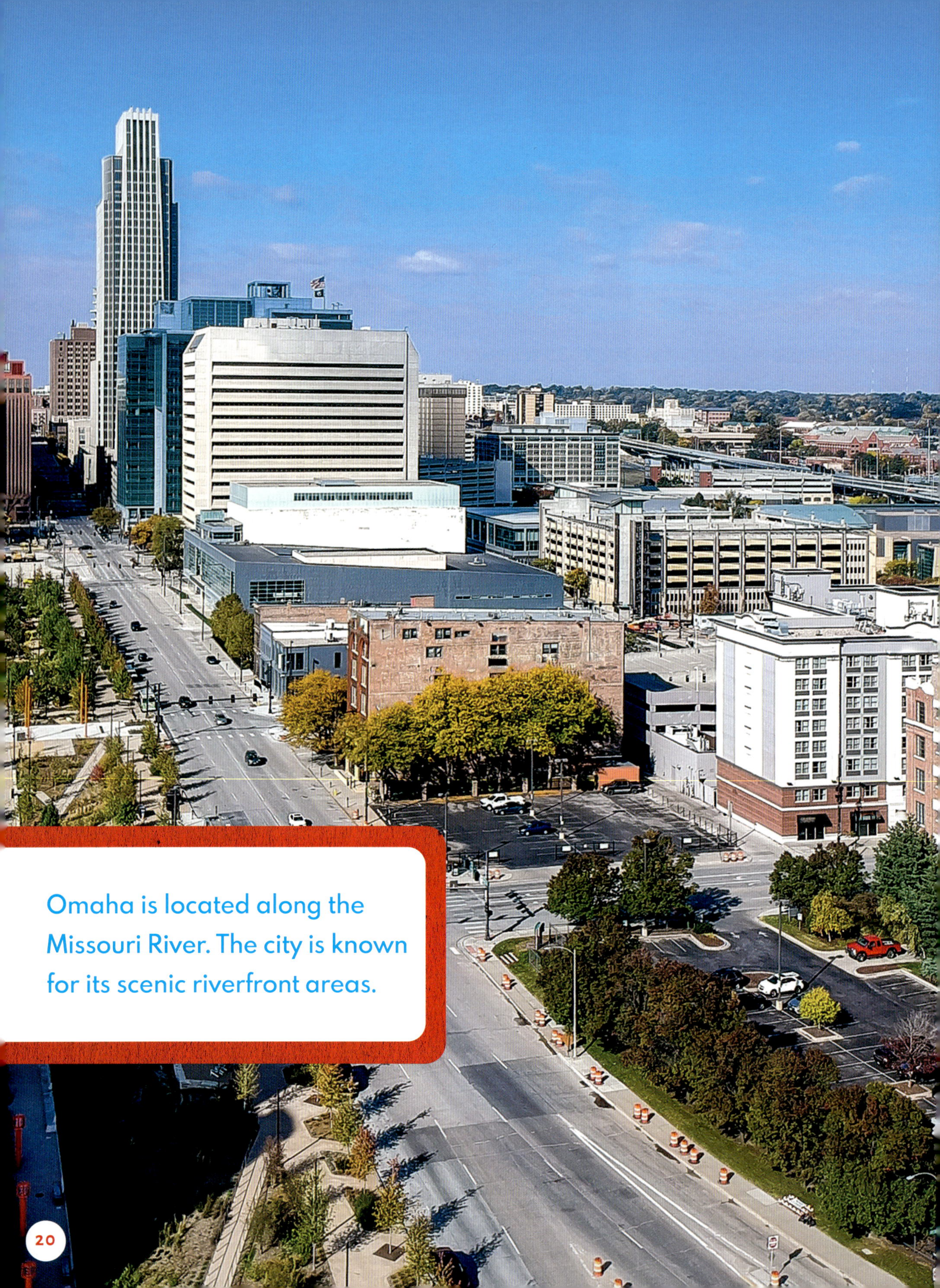

Omaha is located along the Missouri River. The city is known for its scenic riverfront areas.

Places in Nebraska

The capital of Nebraska is Lincoln. But Omaha is the state's largest city. Other important cities in Nebraska include Bellevue and Grand Island. The Nebraska State Fair is held every year in Grand Island.

Parks

Nebraska has several national park sites. One is Scotts **Bluff** National Monument. It features hiking trails and large rock formations. The site was an important stop for settlers traveling west. At Agate Fossil Beds National Monument, visitors learn about the history of Nebraska's land. People can see fossils that were discovered at the site.

Nebraska also has several state parks. People can hike, camp, and bike at Platte River State Park. They can see a waterfall and climb a man-made tower. At Indian Cave State Park, visitors can explore a cave. It has very old American Indian rock carvings on its walls.

Scotts Bluff rises 800 feet (244 m) above the ground. It was an important landmark for people traveling across the Great Plains.

Fort Robinson State Park features a historic fort. It was used from the 1800s to the 1940s. The park includes hiking trails and a museum. It is also home to longhorn cattle and bison.

The Nebraska State Capitol building has a dome and statue on top of its main tower.

Landmarks

In Lincoln, visitors can see the Nebraska State Capitol building. It was completed in 1932 and includes a big tower. People can also visit the museum at Fairview. This was once the home of William Jennings Bryan, a famous **orator** and politician. He lived at Fairview in the early 1900s. Visitors can learn about Bryan's life and career.

Nebraska and the Oregon Trail

The Oregon Trail passes through Nebraska. Between the 1840s and 1880s, thousands of settlers traveled across the United States on this trail. Robidoux Pass is a gap in Nebraska's Wildcat Hills. The pass provided a place for travelers to rest. Today, the Oregon Trail is a National Historic Trail.

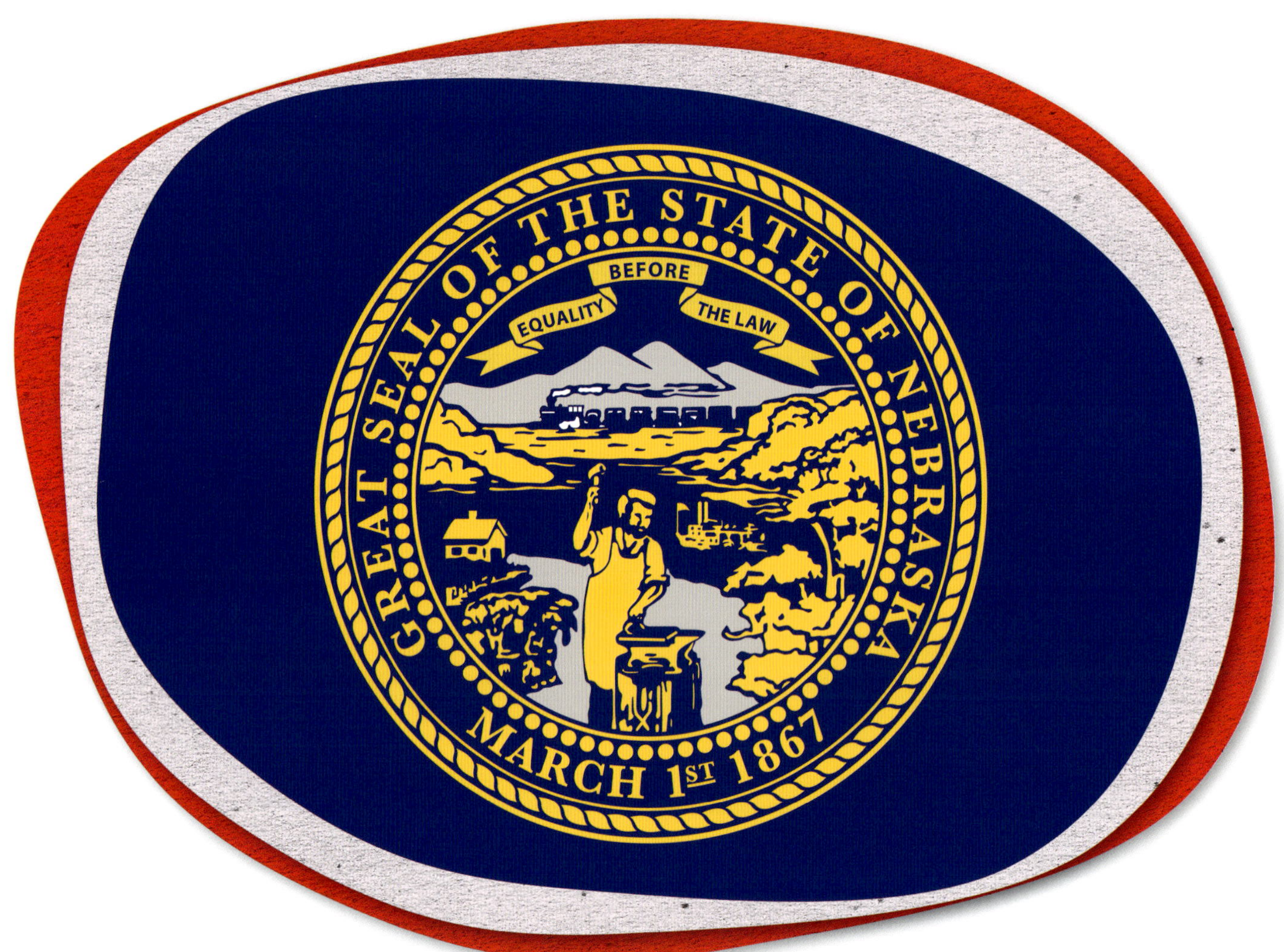

Nebraska's state flag features images of a settler, a steamboat, and a train.

In Omaha, people can tour the Great Plains Black History Museum. It is located in a historic building. The museum focuses on the achievements of Black Americans in the Great Plains area.

Nebraska is a state full of adventures. People can enjoy beautiful state parks and landmarks. They can learn about the state's history at museums. Nebraska has something for everyone.

Explore Online

Look at the website below. Does it give any new evidence to support Chapter Three?

Scotts Bluff National Monument

abdocorelibrary.com/discovering-nebraska

State Map

Omaha

KEY

Capital
Park
City or town
Point of interest

Platte River State Park

Nebraska: The Cornhusker State

South Dakota
Wyoming
Agate Fossil Beds National Monument
Niobrara River
Missouri River
Fort Robinson State Park
Iowa
SAND HILLS
Scotts Bluff National Monument
Lake McConaughy
North Platte
Omaha
Bellevue
Lincoln
Grand Island
Colorado
Platte River
Platte River State Park
National Willa Cather Center
Indian Cave State Park
Missouri
Kansas
N
W
E
S

Scotts Bluff National Monument

Glossary

bluff
a steep hill, cliff, or bank

droughts
periods of little or no rainfall

fossil
the very old, preserved remains of an animal or plant

fur trappers
people who hunt and trap animals and trade their furs

humid
describing air that has a lot of moisture

manufacturing
the process of making goods to sell

orator
a skilled public speaker

reservations
lands set aside by a government for a specific group of people

Online Resources

To learn more about Nebraska, visit our free resource websites below.

Visit **abdocorelibrary.com** or scan this QR code for free Common Core resources for teachers and students, including vetted activities, multimedia, and booklinks, for deeper subject comprehension.

Visit **abdobooklinks.com** or scan this QR code for free additional online weblinks for further learning. These links are routinely monitored and updated to provide the most current information available.

Learn More

Cooper, Robert. *Nebraska Cornhuskers.* Abdo, 2021.

Murray, Julie. *Nebraska.* Abdo, 2020.

Walker, Cameron. *National Monuments of the USA.* Wide Eyed Editions, 2023.

Index

About the Author

Joanne Mattern is the author of many books for young readers. Her favorite topics include history, geography, biography, and science. She loves sharing information with her readers and helping them discover new things. Mattern lives in New York with her family.